The Softest Part of a Woman Is a Wound

poems by

Suzanne Richardson

Finishing Line Press
Georgetown, Kentucky

The Softest Part of a Woman
Is a Wound

Copyright © 2016 by Suzanne Richardson
ISBN 978-1-944899-21-9 First Edition
All rights reserved under International and Pan-American Copyright Conventions.
No part of this book may be reproduced in any manner whatsoever without written permission from the publisher, except in the case of brief quotations embodied in critical articles and reviews.

ACKNOWLEDGMENTS

"When Cleaning Out the Closet I Find Your Needles", *Vending___ Machine* Press, April 2015

"Woman Beside I-25 North", "How it Ends" *Mas Tequila Review*, August 2014

"Utica High," *Two Cities Review*, Spring 2014, Issue 1

"Woman in Alley: Flaggstaff, Arizona," "Crying Woman in Apartment Next Door: Albuquerque, New Mexico," *Sundog Lit* 2014

"Woman on Dirt Road: Taos, New Mexico," *Prick of the Spindle,* Issue 8.1 March 2014

"Rabbit Season," "Fire Season," "Learn the Dark," "Poems For My Lover's Unborn Child Out West," *Booth Journal,* May 2013

"Valley Fever," *Blood Orange Review,* Winter 2011 Volume 6.4

"Reversing Candle," "Arkansas," *The Smoking Poet*, Spring 2012

"The Curse," "The Cursed," *PANK Magazine,* May 2012

Editor: Christen Kincaid

Cover Art: Alexandria Marie Compo

Author Photo: Carol B. Richardson

Cover Design: Elizabeth Maines

Printed in the USA on acid-free paper.
Order online: www.finishinglinepress.com
also available on amazon.com

Author inquiries and mail orders:
Finishing Line Press
P. O. Box 1626
Georgetown, Kentucky 40324
U. S. A.

Table of Contents

Reversing Candle 1
Woman in Alley: Flagstaff, Arizona 2
Crying Woman in the Apartment Next Door: Albuquerque, New Mexico 3
Woman Beside I-25 North: Between Albuquerque and Santa Fe 4
Woman on Dirt Road: Taos, New Mexico 6
Woman in Arroyo: Santa Fe, New Mexico 7
Boys Bathroom 8
Arkansas 9
The Curse 11
The Cursed 12
Rabbit Season 13
Fire Season 14
Poems for My Lover's Unborn Child Out West 15
Valley Fever 18
Something Burned 20
Utica High 22
When Cleaning Out The Closet I Find Your Needles 24
Learn The Dark 25
Walk Through The Doorways 26

Dedicated in Memory of Roger B. Smith

Reversing Candle

Because I feel poison-sad
I light a candle and the black birds come.
They fill the tree with their
dead flesh cries; rotten apple brains, they
count the days of winter in me.
Those I've wronged, those
that wronged me wipe
the slate clean. I pray for teeth to bite
a new tongue. I pray the wild cats leave.
Let the candle worry black for me.
Red night to light
send it back.

Make it like a crocus
growing verso towards the bulb,
or a doe at dawn
running backwards
through a graveyard
only its hooves knowing
we must cross the dead to forgive the living.

Woman in Alley: Flagstaff, Arizona

I used to be like you, swelling—purple under
my milk dress. A tooth fell out every time I let a man
core me. Once they get in, there's nothing—boring holes
is an ecstasy, a garden. Look, there one goes—Lord,
save us from his circular hunger. I am too much of a desert
to receive but I still want the water. My breasts are crushed
petals. I will drink gasoline. I will open my coat, show
you where it hurts. I followed every man
who colored a map up my thigh—Beware!
At the center of all men is a deep smoke. Don't be
like me: the bull rider who only feels complete
the moment he's been gored.

Crying Woman in the Apartment Next Door: Albuquerque, New Mexico

—I lie
on top of him
and feel
myself grow
strange a
crow's claw
caught on the nest, a
blade of grass
blue-dull at the
root no man
is bigger than
my own dark
hole beside
the coffee table
I am dead now
sleeping
next to him
is a gun I
never wanted
what's left of
2am? Can't we fix it?
the way I stretched
myself thin on him
a stream of maple
syrup

Woman beside I-25 North: Between Albuquerque and Santa Fe

I am the skinny cat; lick
hot tar off my bones, my
sticky body. Pick
me up in that truck and
I'll be quiet in my blue jeans.
The figure eight of my ass
makes you strike like
a milk snake. I can get loud.
Bend me—drive
into that bend up the
hill. Blast through rock
to make a road, make it
jagged/smooth.

I've been inside
where the women are starving pieces
of glass—we cut
anything we touch. Don't let me starve—
When I was a girl, someone
fed me honeycomb until
I threw up. The dark hairy knuckles
of a man's hand,
pressing my tongue. Don't
you know the softest part of
 a woman is a wound?

Speed up,
I am the fastest kitty.
I want to ride. Imagine my hair
turning colors in your
mouth, black/brown/blonde.
Each time you think you know me
I'll change— first you'll like it, then
you'll hump/dump me
by the side of the road, like
every other rotten coyote who
caught my scent and
had to stop and lick.

Woman on Dirt Road: Taos, New Mexico

Know this, owls are doors.
They travel where we cannot.
Don't let the wind blow through
your ears or the owls will point
out the dead. Some among us died
long ago but they still walk. When I was a girl
the owls tried to take me. One owl flew
into my window, broke
its neck. My grandmother ran
to my room and shook salt on my bed. Prayed
all night for me, but
it was my brother who
never came home. He was face
down in a creek, his mouth full
of worms and silt.
They took him.
Once, I sat by a tree at sixteen
my body cramping,
and an owl howled as I lost my daughter:
small, slick, screech of flesh
in my underwear—
the garlic bloom of my cervix
opened and closed. I know
what you're thinking, but only a woman would
call another woman a witch.
It has always been this way—
I am no longer afraid of
the messages they bring,
I've lived long now. Next
I see one, I will let it in.

Woman in Arroyo: Santa Fe, New Mexico

—*Mal de ojo*—I smell it—*un Diablo,*
the stench on your back. Suck the
soup bones. Braid
precious herbs and
onion skins into your hair. Taste
with your tongue the fresh fat of the milk.
You must cook a rabbit slow   skin on—
You should watch
windows for signs of evil. Increase
your blessings with
orange peels in your
bed. If the eye stays on you
take pony hair and
thread through it some gold charms
or teeth. If the fear is worse at night drink only
from a turtle shell. This is a wish
for your fortune. Someone
wants what you have. They
have grown jealous
like short trees in the forest, and so
you must put two needles
in a bowl of water. Drop the oil
ojo contra ojo for ten days will
burst the curse. You will
know when it's gone;
you will wake up with the taste
of fruit in your mouth. Your
whole life, fated
 as it once was
in the cosmos. Like
the pink of a shell
in the wax and crook
of your palm.

Boys Bathroom

bhhy—And I said 'Buena madre' but she said
I was bad, bad, bad, and I said
I got lots of rats runnin' around here who like me.
One time in the boys bathroom I saw how they did—
different than how I did. They said they'd teach me and
I told them we'd better not. That's when the fuss
started and my skirt lifted up. I say, we were just kids,
just rats runnin' around. It don't make me any less Buena.

Arkansas

Boy Dog in the yard, Nollie Gray
in the hen house. Someone's
wringing a chicken's neck, or did someone
wring her neck? Someone plucked her feathers
until she was naked on train tracks.
Her fear, like a stone hits
a tin roof and whatever she saw, she saw.
Whatever she says happened,
happened—but, she only tells
 the stitches in the quilt. She irons over it
like linens and table lace. Blue it out but I know
something is wrong because she
put my hand on a map and showed me
Arkansas. She put
my hands in the catfish waters of Arkansas. I think,
two sticks rubbed together and
lit her up like tobacco flowers and ragweed
in Arkansas. Whatever happened,
I'll bury it for her. Along with the
dead dogs and
smashed pennies. I'll hopscotch over it,
pick up the jax—
I was told, believe in the church of Arkansas!
Though it baptized her with the snakes.
Believe in the church of Arkansas!
Though it cut the puppy tails.
Believe in the church of Arkansas!
Where a man spat Coca-Cola
on the pulpit moving like Elvis.
Where she believed it was God's hand reaching
up her skirt, until it happened on a Monday.
I think, like a cow, she grew

a second stomach to digest what happened. But Lord,
don't let her pass down this unknown bag
of bones. Bathe her in the wheelbarrow—
let the water be an apology
let the rag confirm she was dirty.
In the hell of her past I root for her,
burnt garbage, rusty nails. I glean the rows
of her crops. I lick the smut,
pick the meat, gnaw
that riverbank, to know what she tasted.
I'm trying to show her, I know something
happened. When she feels like screaming I want her to
open my mouth, and pour Arkansas in.

The Curse

I pray this thorn pushes through me
into you. I ask poison to press
upon your palms and knees. I hope for
your permanent brown. Let the universe
feed you stones until your garden grows
sick with weeds.

The Cursed

I awoke with snow in my mouth, diamond snakeskin between my legs. A small sooty shadow fell on my cheek I tried to wipe it but bone-hands held it over my head. I felt as small as a cherry pit, my insides turning like a rotten melon. I searched the skies for a sign but my senses grew gray-blue like the silver of a newborn kitten's eyeball; glass-veined and useless. I listened for the voice of my lover, my mother, but all I heard were worms eating their way through the crust of this dirty earth.

Rabbit Season

Years before we met, we
                      imagined the same rabbit
thumping a salt bush—*conejo* you
                              whispered deep into
your desk drawer, the sound split
                              my head, like how
a rock diverts rivers. I
                am your thorny
little sister not your lover. I
                    watched you jump
at every skirt but mine. Later, I
                          throw up green in your Juniper bush
while your lover tells me I
                    am so good, so quiet when I
reveal what's inside. Brother,
                      last I heard, you watched a rabbit die
its head bashed purple on a fence post,
                          it was something I couldn't imagine.

Fire Season

In moth season I levitate because of a married man,
the sound of my own desire keeps
me awake at night, keeps me tossing four-feet
above the sheets, I imagine us powder-thrashing
like moths at a screen—

On the roof of his car, off route 14,
it feels like 1955. We watch the moon squeeze itself
between the earth and the sun. It's
hallucinatory, the sun is a shrinking slice of light.
We
can't touch. I am already casting hell-grey shadows,
eclipsing his wife. It's so devastating
we must not look directly.
His voice, *If I live my life right, I'll die on the moon
looking at the earth,
looking at all the people I love, and all the people
I once loved.* A married man
pushes the atmosphere and I levitate above
the forest, this moth season behind me,
he murmurs—*soon this will all be on fire.*

Poems for My Lover's Unborn Child out West

The moment he created you,
he said, was an ending. His
ending triggered you. Like
a scream into a canyon,
you are the echo back, a ricochet,
a likeness of
his sound blended, spattered out
on the canyon walls, then,
turning the corner,
coming back to him.

*

Since he rubbed you
into another woman, I float you
my thistle milk whenever I wish
you had been my bead.

*

I know her body
wasn't strange like mine and
therefore, a home. But you would
have liked it here. I have
soft wood floors and hard ripe
apples. Did you even try?

*

You are not yet a star
but you already make enough light
for me to see that I was/am lost.

*

You are a hot coil;
you cook me,
cook him, but you
don't yet speak the language
of burns.

*

When I get upset
I sing you a lullaby:
I rock you, rock you
until you sleep. Your
mother keeps you, keeps you
and I weep.

*

He wove you into her
while I was away.
You are small, breathing
only your mother's soup;
your gills, a delicate, light, lace;
moving, mirroring, how I open
then close the door when
I ask him to leave.

*

Shhh—listen closely,
a star burns
brightest
right before
it dies and you
are that moment, little one.

       *

A birthday gift to you: I
fade   so far   east,
I am   another country,
another
      century, another
galaxy away—
—promise   me   your   first
breath   will
erase/release   me.

Valley Fever

After it was done, I put a shirt on,
A fungus grows in the spine.
Valley Fever. Father is dying;

might die.
I took a sip, asked him what he did
some story here—
a funeral home,
a hearse,
a flesh eating disease, and

a mask just in case.
He says: People don't die like they used to.
He means: You're alive, so touch me.
Valley Fever lodges in the lung,
a sporophyte in the heart, skin, bones.
I do things, to myself

fertilize my own pain with him.
Let the gametes meet with him.
He walked me to my car,
let his mouth bloom over mine.
Once, he worked inside a freezer
in an ice cream shop,
and it made him cold.
He raised an eyebrow—
what was my excuse?

I reach out for him,
then let him go.
What happens when you only do things once?
After him, I was hidden,

unbeautiful, concave. The reason
I'm disintegrating,
a reason I might disintegrate.

Something Burned

I could hear the bugs, the Chhh-Chhh—
chattering as they ate it, the
last bit of it out in the yard—

Could you hear it too?

The things feeding on
our dead love. They ate us apart.

My neighbor came out
to see the sound.

Did someone birth a child?   Lose a child?   a dead child?

She asked me, in the dark
pointing to the turf.

                              I'm sorry, I responded,

        it's not that urgent. But part of me

felt flattered. It wasn't just us,

it was affecting others too
like a bad smell,

or a bomb. My neighbor's still dark form
a friend in that most lonely
hour.

I see, she said,   *Yours smells like*
orange peels, and
gasoline, and leather. Mine smelled like
sex and mold. No matter what it
always, always, always, smells
like a body
and the absence
of a body.

Good luck with this.

She went back inside the door.

In the morning our dead

love turned to smoke.

what was ignited?

who set it on fire?

I know something burned.

Utica High

It's me and Franco Franco and we're laugh rattling in the back of chemistry class like a pair of rotten tomatoes, like two tennis shoes tied together, like telephone cord curled in on itself, like the horizontal red white and green the other boys see when we punch their socks out.

It's me and Franco Franco and we're crammed in his sick-ass yellow mustang, our eyes watering, our cocks growing like hot commas against our jeans as we look at all the boom-boom babies at the burger joint, all the Mary Maries, and the Angelinas, and the Monicas with their pasta nest hair and their Our Father asses, and their spaghetti strap tops.

And it's me and Franco Franco on his Ma's white-white couch and he's such a cugine the way he rolls up his track pants, the way he says a Hail Mary faster than anyone, the way he's always got another Fuck Your Mother inside him, the way he's knee deep in the tomato pie in the middle of the night, the way he combs his hair with a knife.

It's me and Franco Franco and we're army crawling past midnight under his mother's lace table cloth, breaking her crystal water glasses with our pelvic movements, we're just trying to get out, get into something, get on top of something and we're shaking the table the one with all the other Francos on it, their portraits: wide-eyed Nona Franco and loosey goosey Jimmy Franco, and wing tipped Geno Franco, and baby Francesca Franco who grew up a straight-up beauty bomb. The Franco chins, all moving, all wagging, all watching—they're gonna rat on us, rat us out, we are rats Franco Franco and I—we moved so slow, I swear, I swear, we saw the holy ghost.

When Cleaning Out the Closet I Find Your Needles

Next to a photo album, a shoebox full of mixtapes, a lock of my hair— is your portal glowing like a neon in a liquor store window: OPEN the metal blinks. The door to your other life is ajar as I hold them in my hands, like monster's teeth, like jewels from outer space, like long stem roses; thorns still on. Boundary lines on a map that mark the parts of you where I have not been, the parts of you, you grow in the dark, the parts of you that sleep whenever I am awake, the parts of you that come out by the dim single bulb of our square bathroom light, your eyes sloshing with tears, your tongue slow and deep and plunging in my throat, plunging in yours. You are the slowest fish when you shoot up, a gentle body of water. I am on the couch next to the ocean. I am drowning in a hot blue liquid. I am weeping into you, we are salt water, a blind bed of eels biting each other for warmth. Your veins are open tonight and when you talk pieces of blue fall out. Hooks in your arm you filet yourself. You are the doctor and the patient and you always need more medicine. Only on the other side can you see yourself clearly and you can't see me at all. The saline of your soul blurring.

You are the deepest rabbit hole, the scariest ride at the carnival, and when I tell you this, you say, *I love you, I love you, get off.*

Learn the Dark

I haunt
the streets where I wonder if
my former lovers feel my
planetary pull. I am trapped between
two moons: you tell me if I were a man
and you were a woman you'd
let me touch your body tonight. I feel
my own fish squirming, and
your hands, batwings, pulse and
peel open—
we don't touch.
I go to the graveyard searching for meaning.
I go to hear all the death: little Eliza Olin, gone
since 1832, and me so alive; I must spook her.
Then—
—body noise: breath   moving
liquid.
And I hear all the life:
the orgasms blinking outward
 like rescue signals at dawn. Men fucking
by the precious headstones of the orphans.
a slip, a grind, a burn, okay—
Only when I am this thirsty do I
drink the spit of strangers. Later, I
dreamt your wet stretches
of saliva fell into me; you
let the bulbs burn out, opened
your mouth, and let me learn the dark.

Walk Through the Doorways

If you choose to walk through the doorways
You will become less   of a mystery to yourself.
Do not—and you will boil   like broth in a pot, hot
     by an unknown hand.

First, eliminate what the self is not.
               Things that are not you will not survive the
doorways—will not come with you.   You are not a lung it
                              contracts *for*
you, not *as* you.   Are you a mind? You are not, but this is closer
to what you really are.
          You are not your springing thoughts—you are an
observer as they   pulse and grow.
You are much smaller, less regal than a lung, a kernel, a hairy root,
a stone,   —that kind of constant   is you.
                    Things that are not constant   are
not   you.

You must prepare to walk through the doorways.
                         If you do not, you will be
shattered.   Trapped.   Unknowable. Even oracles   will
not predict the suffering   that will write itself
                    on the smallness of you.   You
cannot bring   control   it will fall like sand onto the metal of you.
                              You
must prepare to stretch   without ripping.
                         Practice the stretch—
     sleep parallel to the doorways, sleep and wake in prayer to
the doorways   bend every cell in their direction.   You must give
                              up landscapes for
the rich pathways inside.

When you are ready   walk to the tree line   the portal—the
                          spruces, dappled along the pond—
To the left extends your mind,   your   deepest, truest, self
that   Freudian reservoir, an artifact collecting dust
in the basement
                of
Yourself.   To the right is the longest mirror—the pond,
                                         that body of water,
your kin that casts shadows in   your body, a cellular
ship that
sails
out and out and out into— a universe. Magic
                        is an inner science, do not push on
the doorways to open them.   you must push
                             from within   to walk
through the doorways.

Suzanne Richardson was born and raised in Durham, North Carolina, where she received an alternative education at Carolina Friends School K-12. She then graduated from Bard College in 2005 with a degree in English and Creative Writing. Suzanne earned her MFA in Albuquerque, New Mexico at the University of New Mexico. She currently lives in Utica, New York where she is an Assistant Professor of English at Utica College where she teaches English and creative writing. Suzanne was editor-in-chief of Blue Mesa Review from 2010-2012. Her nonfiction has appeared in *New Ohio Review, New Haven Review, The Journal,* and *Prime Number Magazine.* Her fiction has appeared in *Front Porch, MAYDAY Magazine, High Desert Journal,* and *Southern Humanities Review.* Her poetry has appeared in *Prick of the Spindle, Sundog Lit, Mas Tequila Review, Blood Orange Review, The Smoking Poet, PANK Magazine* and *BOOTH.* She is currently working on a memoir.

www.ingramcontent.com/pod-product-compliance
Lightning Source LLC
Chambersburg PA
CBHW060226050426
42446CB00013B/3193